Dolphin Babies

Making A Splash

Diane Sweeney and Michelle Reddy
Photographs by Jeff Smith
Cartoons by Jim Corey

ROBERTS RINEHART PUBLISHERS
Boulder, Colorado

This book celebrates the love and dedication of the trainers and veterinarians without whom none of this would have been possible. It is to these caring individuals that we dedicate this book.

Published by Roberts Rinehart Publishers
6309 Monarch Park Place
Niwot, Colorado 80503

Distributed to the trade by Publishers Group West

Published in Ireland and the U.K. by
Roberts Rinehart Publishers
Trinity House, Charleston Road
Dublin 6, Ireland

Text copyright © 1998 by Diane Sweeney and Michelle Reddy
Photographs copyright © 1998 by Jeff Smith
Cartoons by Jim Corey

Cover design: Ann W. Douden
Interior design and production: Jill Soukup

International Standard Book Number 1-57098-194-9
Library of Congress Cataloging in Publication data:

Sweeney, Diane.
    Dolphin babies : making a splash / Diane Sweeney, Michelle Reddy.
        p. cm.
    Includes bibliographical references.
    Summary: Chronicles the birth and development of four bottlenose
dolphin calves and the growth of three of them to their first birthday.
        ISBN 1-57098-194-9 (pbk.)
        1. Bottlenosed dolphins—Infancy-Juvenile literature.
    [1. Bottlenosed dolphins. 2. Dolphins. 3. Animals—Infancy.]
    I. Reddy, Michelle. II. Title.
    QL737.C432S84 1998
    599.53'3139—DC21   97-46591
                                                       CIP
                                                       AC

Printed in Hong Kong through Phoenix Offset, Ltd.

Contents

Introduction—4

Dolphin Babies—7

Tell Me More About Dolphins—58

Authors' Note—60

Suggested Reading for Young People—61

Annotated Bibliography—62

Acknowledgments—64

Introduction

This is the story of four adult female bottlenose dolphins, Kona, Leilani, Pele, and Shaka, who each had her first calf during one remarkable summer. The calves, three male and one female, were all born within thirteen days in the protected lagoon of Dolphin Quest on the Big Island of Hawaii. This book chronicles the development and birth of these calves and the growth of three of them to their first birthday.

The Dolphin Quest facility is a large, pristine natural habitat for bottlenose dolphins located at the Hilton Waikoloa Village on the Kona Coast. In this beautiful environment, children, teens, and adults are able to meet and interact with the dolphins. Such special personal experiences promote appreciation for these fascinating and charming creatures and help to engender a sense of stewardship for our oceans.

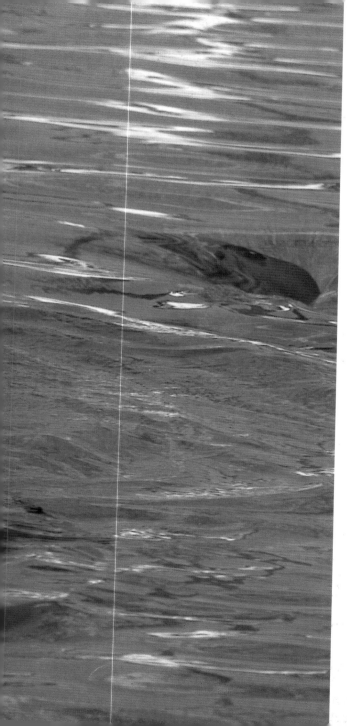

Dolphin Babies

Meet Kona. Kona is an energetic female Atlantic bottlenose dolphin, *Tursiops truncatus*. She lives with the rest of her Dolphin Quest family, Leilani, Pele, Shaka, Hobi, and Lono, at the beautiful Dolphin Learning Center Lagoon at the Hilton Waikoloa Village on the Big Island of Hawaii. Because they live in Hawaii, all the dolphins at Dolphin Quest have Hawaiian names. Kona was named for the nearby town of Kona.

Leilani

Pele

Leilani, Pele, and Shaka are also females. Leilani is Hawaiian for heavenly flower, Pele is the Hawaiian goddess of the volcano, and Shaka is the Hawaiian sign for hang loose.

The two males are Hobi and Lono. Lono is Hawaiian for god of harvest, and Hobi has a dorsal fin that looks like the sail on a Hobi Cat sailboat.

Shaka

Lono

Hobi

9

*F*emale dolphins can be old enough to have babies when they are six years old. Males can sometimes become fathers when they are as young as eight years but usually they are older, more like 10 to 13. In the summer of 1993, all the dolphins were nine years old. So it wasn't surprising to find out that all four female dolphins, Leilani, Pele, Kona, and Shaka, were pregnant. But who were the fathers?

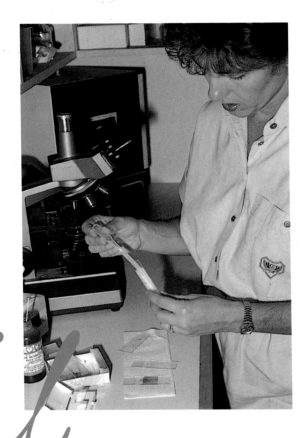

sing blood tests and other exams, the veterinarians at Dolphin Quest learned that Lono was not grown up enough to be a father, but Hobi was. Therefore, Hobi was soon to be the proud papa of all four babies!

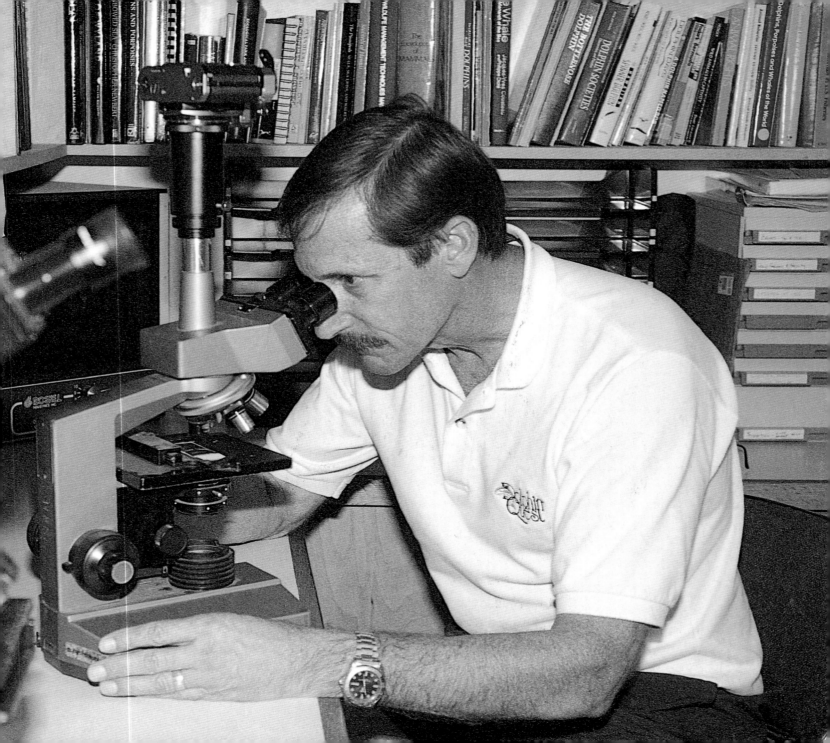

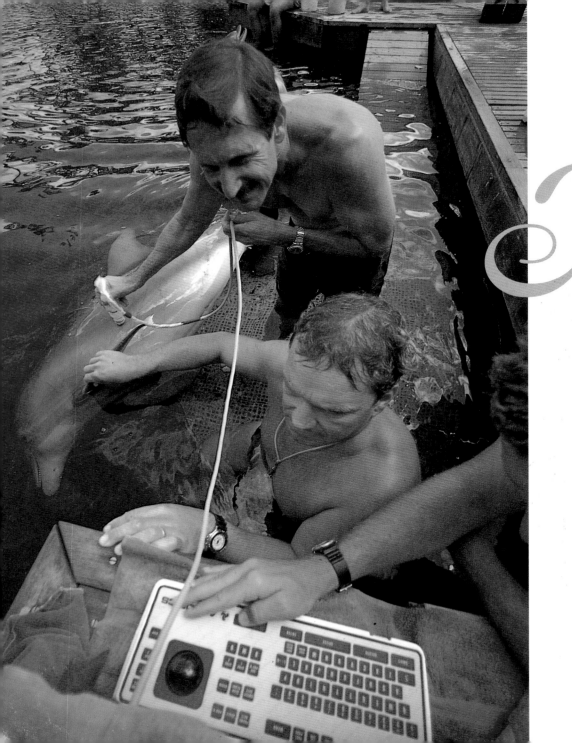

To monitor the dolphins' pregnancies, the veterinarians used ultrasound. Ultrasound is the same tool used to monitor the development of human babies. The dolphins' trainers taught them to float quietly beside the dock so they would be comfortable during examinations. Then veterinarians could use the ultrasound imaging machine to "see" the developing baby, which is called a fetus at the early stages of growth. At about six weeks of age, the developing fetuses were the size of a peanut.

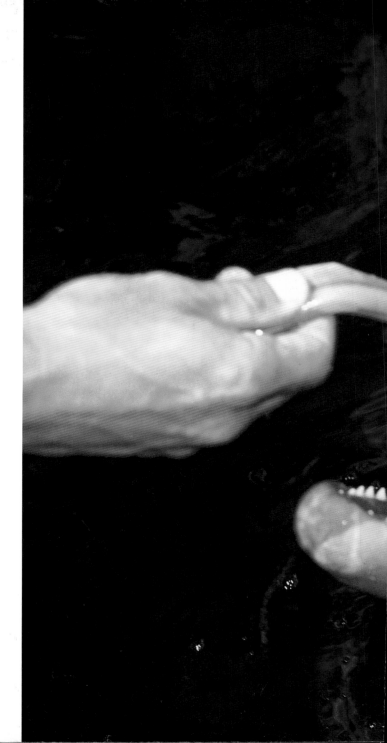

*P*regnancy lasts about 12 months for bottlenose dolphins. In the first months, the expectant moms did not require any special treatment. They continued to eat their balanced diet of restaurant-quality seafood: herring, smelt, capelin, mackerel, and squid. They continued with their normal schedule of play, rest, and training.

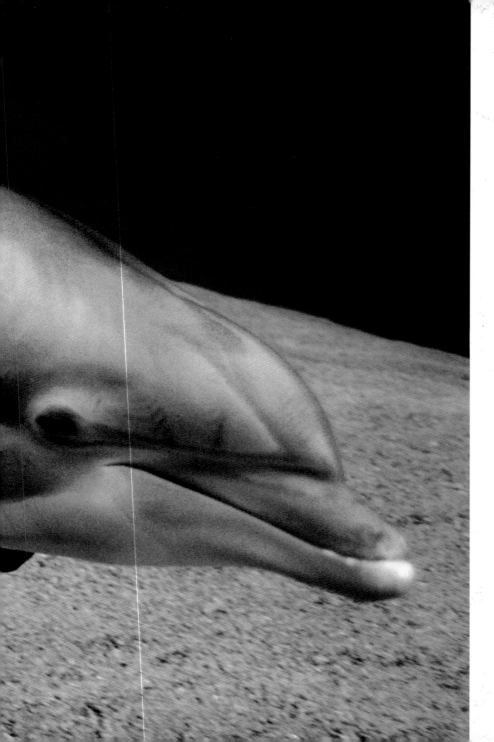

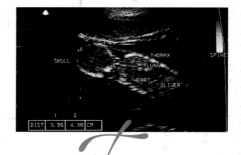

The pregnant dolphins also received regular check-ups by the veterinarians. Every month, the veterinarians would use the ultrasound machine to watch the progress of the developing fetuses. They could identify many body parts, like the head and heart. They took pictures and kept detailed records of every ultrasound exam, and they made measurements of certain parts of the developing fetus so they could learn more about the dolphins and share it with other scientists. This kind of information is not available from studies in the wild. The dolphins seemed to enjoy the attention and rubdowns they got during their ultrasound exams. Even the males wanted a turn!

*I*t is a sad fact that with most mammals, their first-born will not live to be one year old. This is also true for bottlenose dolphins, whose babies are called calves. In a population of wild dolphins in Florida, one out of every five calves born did not live to see its first birthday. Of the calves whose mothers were inexperienced or younger than 15 years old, less than one-half survived to become independent. The others died from drowning, illness, and predators such as sharks. In the wild, mothers have to protect their calves from sharks, sometimes by bringing them to a dolphin "nursery area" where the water is rather shallow and there are lots of fish to play with and eat, but not many sharks.

One of the first things newborn calves have to learn is how to suckle their mother's rich milk UNDER WATER! First-time dolphin mothers have to learn how to feed their calves like this. To make sure the first-time Dolphin Quest mothers would know how to nurse their calves, the trainers used a rubber dolphin puppet to simulate a suckling calf. This type of training has been successful with many animals in zoos, including gorillas and other primates.

Dolphin milk comes from a nipple that is tucked inside a small slit. Each female dolphin has two slits, one on either side of the genital opening. To begin, the trainers taught the dolphin mothers to turn their bodies toward the dolphin puppet that was on the trainer's hand.

Next, the puppet was moved in the water so the dolphins would learn how to suckle while swimming. The mother dolphins were also taught to present their mammary slits to the trainers. This behavior would allow the trainers to collect milk from the dolphins after the birth of the calves. Then the milk could be stored in case one of the calves had to be raised by hand.

Scientists think that the milk produced soon after birth is very important for newborns. This first milk has special proteins called immunoglobulins that help protect the young from disease. Similar proteins can be found in dolphin blood. So, a blood sample was collected from Hobi and sent to a laboratory where the immunoglobulins were taken from the blood and stored in case they were needed.

*T*he closer they came to the due date, the larger the expectant moms grew. They had each gained about 100 pounds. They seemed to enjoy resting their bellies on the soft sand of the shallow beach for short periods of time throughout the day and night. About a month before the births of the calves were expected, everyone began to prepare for the event. A veterinarian was on watch 24 hours a day, the trainers put off their vacations and stopped by on their days off; even the security guards were extra alert. By the end of the month, the staff was tired and tense, excited and eager, anxious but guarded.

In a study of wild dolphins off the coast of Florida, scientists found that calves are usually born from late spring through early summer, when the water is the warmest. On the last day of June at Dolphin Quest, Pele began to show the first signs of labor. She seemed agitated and wasn't interested in food. Her genital opening was swollen, and once in a while, a white stream of milk was seen coming from her mammary slits. This was finally what we had been waiting for — Pele was in labor!

*L*ate that afternoon, Pele was observed to be having periodic contractions. She swam slowly, pausing while her body shuddered with the force of normal contractions of labor. Cameras were poised, but filming the birth became a dim possibility at sunset as the sun slipped beneath the shimmering Hawaiian sea. The staff watched and waited, allowing nature to take its course as it has for thousands of years. Everything and everybody was ready and alert in case Pele or her new calf needed help.

*I*t is very rare and difficult for people to see the actual birth or even the first few days of life for a baby dolphin in the wild. Scientists rely on observations made at marine mammal facilities such as Dolphin Quest. On this night, more than 200 people, from Hawaii and throughout the world, waited at the lagoon and watched for many hours. The air was electric in anticipation of this miracle of birth.

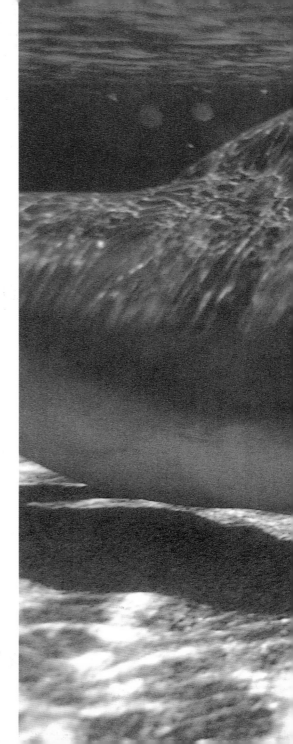

*A*t 9 o'clock in the evening, a strong contraction resulted in the sudden exposure of one of the calf's flukes. Birth was close! Because dolphins need air to breathe, most dolphins are born flukes first. With each contraction, the soft little flukes flopped back and forth, and more of the calf's body could be seen. Pele swam energetically now, sometimes rubbing her belly on the sandy floor of the lagoon. She also swam close to her trainers in the shallow water for rubdowns. With one final explosive thrust at 10:50 P.M., the tiny calf was finally born!

ele swam around the lagoon, producing a wake that pulled the newborn calf beside her. One time the calf headed up the beach, but the trainers headed it back toward its mother. Soon the other females were swimming with Pele and the newborn, carefully watching the exciting new activity. As a precautionary measure, the males had been removed to an enclosure nearby because male dolphins have been known to sometimes become aggressive with new calves.

Usually, following a normal delivery, the calf will suckle within the first 12 hours. However, this calf did not seem to be responding to Pele's efforts to nurse. Unless nursing began within the first two days, the calf would have no chance to survive on its own. As the hours ticked away, the veterinarians decided to intervene. Although a specially developed dolphin formula with protective immunoglobulins was given to the tiny calf, it died in the early morning. The loss was a tragic blow to everyone, but three more calves were still on the way. Milk was voluntarily collected from Pele, who was eager for the extra attention and willingly provided milk for several days. This was stored in case it was needed by another new calf.

On the Fourth of July, Kona began to have contractions. At 10:48 P.M. she delivered a vigorous little newborn. Kona immediately jostled the calf and began to swim very fast, pulling the calf beside her with her wake. The wrinkled little calf took strong breaths each time it surfaced. Kona was very protective, guiding her calf away from rocks and other objects in the environment. The calf was named Kuokoa, Hawaiian for freedom or independence.

A newborn bottlenose calf weighs about 40 pounds (18 kg) and is about 3 feet long (just over 1 meter). Its first movements are a bit bumpy and stiff, but it quickly gets the hang of smooth movement through the water. By daylight we could tell this calf was nursing! As Kona swam through the lagoon, the little calf nuzzled the genital area where the mammary slits are found. The calf curled its tongue, and the suction it created caused the nipple to come out from the slit. Rich milk poured quickly into the calf's mouth. An entire nursing session took only three to eight seconds, and the calf nursed six to eight times every 10 to 15 minutes.

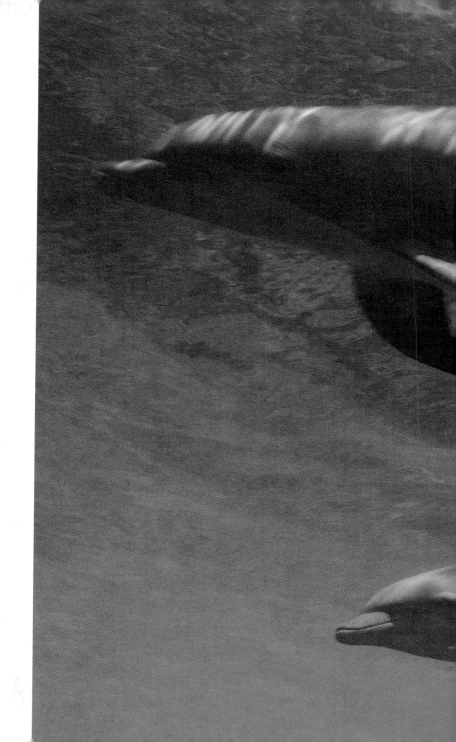

*L*eilani went into labor on July 8th. The ultrasound exams had shown that her baby was slightly smaller than the other calves, so the staff was alerted and prepared for any problems. Happily, Leilani's labor was routine. At 11:58 P.M. her calf was born. The little calf was named Lokahi, Hawaiian for togetherness.

*D*olphin births often happen at night or early morning. Four days after Leilani gave birth, and again in the dark of night, Shaka's calf was born. Shaka's behavior immediately after birth was similar to that of the other dolphins; she bumped her calf about and swam very rapidly, pulling the newborn calf along beside her. Some dolphin experts think that a mother dolphin may jostle the newborn calf to stimulate alertness. By initially pushing it down into deep water, she may cause pressure on the calf's lungs so that when it surfaces it draws in a deep first breath, inflating and activating the lungs. Shaka's calf was named Kolo'he, which means rascal.

*A*ll three mother and calf pairs showed nursing success from the beginning. Within seven to eight hours of birth, each of these calves was suckling strongly. For 24 hours each day, at least one observer monitored the nursery activity. Within a day, we knew that all the calves were males!

ithin a few days of his birth, Shaka's calf was gaining weight and filling out his wrinkled newborn skin. This was normal and healthy development for a calf. However, it surpassed Leilani's calf, Lokahi, who was four days older. Leilani's calf did not seem to be suckling as often, either. It appeared that Leilani might not feel well. By now, Pele had rejoined the group and was acting very motherly with Leilani's calf several times a day. Such a helper is not uncommon and can provide additional protection for the calf. In some cases, a companion female has even nursed a calf that was not her own. Although Pele could provide protection, she was no longer producing milk, so she could not provide nutrition for Leilani's calf.

*T*he veterinarians thought that Leilani might be in the early stages of an infection, so she was promptly given medicine. Antibiotics were put in her fish twice a day. Leilani's calf was given a feeding of dolphin milk that had been collected from Pele. He was also treated with the immunoglobulin concentrate, collected from his dad earlier. Using a gentle tube-feeding procedure developed over the years by facilities caring for dolphins, the veterinarians fed about six ounces of dolphin milk to the calf.

Within a few hours of ingesting the antibiotics, Leilani seemed to feel better. Her calf seemed more energetic, too. Soon Leilani reclaimed her calf from Pele and resumed regular nursing. Thanks to knowledge, skill, and preparation, mother and calf were again doing well.

In the wild, calves ranging in age from three to 13 years will form play groups. The Dolphin Quest babies were also very playful and loved to chase each other and explore the lagoon together. The calves' curiosity and their mothers' tolerance for their explorations were quite remarkable. This kind of very early independence had not been reported before.

$\mathcal{B}$ecause of the well-established trusting relationship between the dolphins and their trainers, the mother dolphins were very relaxed. Within a week, they seemed eager to return to the interactive programs that were an enjoyable part of their days prior to motherhood. The calves seemed interested in all the activities going on in the lagoon, including the human guests interacting with their moms. They soon found out that people were interesting and fun!

Calves in the wild usually don't eat solid food until they are four to 11 months of age. They do seem to enjoy playing a game of cat and mouse with small fish. At 18 to 20 months they will begin to be weaned from their mother's milk. By the time they are about two years old, fish will have become a major part of their diets.

The Dolphin Quest calves often played with little pieces of fish. By the time they were three months old, all three calves were eating two to three pounds of fish each day (about 1 kg) in addition to gulping down their mothers' fat-rich milk.

he trainers introduced "the boys" to various floating toys. The calves quickly learned the secrets of ball control and ring retrieval. These lively youngsters would often zoom over and grab the balls and rings from their mothers and swim off with these prizes.

The dolphin calves were extremely eager to be involved in all aspects of the daily activities at the lagoon. They looked for opportunities to learn. By four months of age, they had already learned nearly a dozen behaviors. They also learned to respond to a trainer's whistle, which signifies a correct response. The whistle says, "YES!" They learned that after the whistle, they would get a rub-down, a cheerful "Good Job!" or a fish treat. Sometimes they learned behaviors by watching and imitating their mothers, but mostly they learned through energetic interactions with the trainers.

*A*t Dolphin Quest, it is very important for the animals to learn behaviors that help with their medical care. By the time they were eight months old, the calves allowed the trainers to collect exhaled breaths, blood samples, and fecal samples. They even held very still while the veterinarian administered the only vaccination necessary for dolphins.

By the time they were nine months old, the calves were extremely interested in the human visitors. The trainers decided to allow them to interact with the human guests for short periods of time, always with careful supervision. The calves were a huge hit! The guests liked the cute antics and boundless energy, and the calves loved all the extra attention.